BALDWIN
DIESEL-ELECTRIC SWITCHING LOCOMOTIVES
OPERATOR'S MANUAL

No. DS-112

750-1000 HP

SWITCHERS & ROAD SWITCHERS

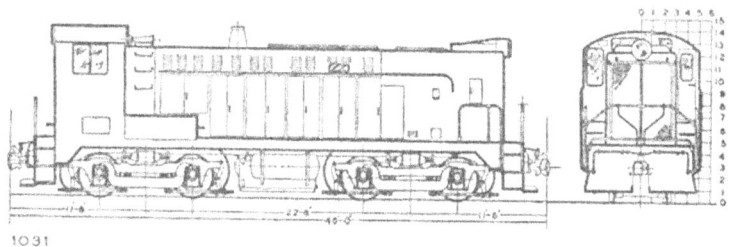

BY
THE BALDWIN LOCOMOTIVE WORKS
PHILADELPHIA, PA.

©2011 Periscope Film LLC
All Rights Reserved
ISBN #978-1-935700-62-3
www.PeriscopeFilm.com

Rev. 5-20-49

DISCLAIMER:
This manual is sold for historic research purposes only, as an entertainment. It contains obselete information and is not intended to be used as part of an actual training program. No book can substitute for proper training by an authorized instructor. The licensing of engineers is overseen by organizations and authorities such as the Federal Railroad Administration. Operating a locomotive without the proper license can result in criminal prosecution.

BALDWIN PAGE 1

CONTENTS

	PAGE
GENERAL SPECIFICATIONS	3
GENERAL DESCRIPTION	5
LOCOMOTIVE OPERATION	10
FUEL OIL SYSTEM	20
LUBRICATING OIL SYSTEM	23
ENGINE COOLING SYSTEM	24
ENGINE OVERSPEED CONTROL	26
CONTROL AIR SYSTEM	26
ELECTRICAL SYSTEM	27
OPERATING DIFFICULTIES	32

LIST OF ILLUSTRATIONS

Fig.		
1.	Switcher	2
2.	750 H.P. Switcher Clearance Diagram	3
3.	1000 H.P. Switcher Clearance Diagram	4
4.	Engineer's Position	6
5.	Equipment Cabinet	7
6.	Cab—Left Side	8
7.	Lube Oil Pump, Strainer, etc.	8
8.	Lube Oil Fill and Gauge	8
9.	Fuel Oil Supply Pump	9
10.	Outside Fuel Cutoff	9
11.	Fuel Tank	9
12.	Diagram of Fuel Oil System	21
13.	Diagram of Lube Oil System	22
14.	Cooling Water System	25
15.	Overspeed Stop	26
16.	Control System Diagram	31

PAGE 2 **BALDWIN**

SWITCHER — Figure 1

BALDWIN PAGE 3

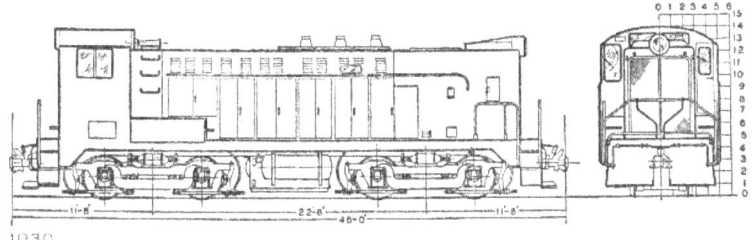

FIGURE 2

750 H. P. SWITCHER

GENERAL SPECIFICATIONS

Driving Wheels, 4 pairs .... 40 inches

Gear Ratio 14:68

Maximum Speed Restriction .... 60 m.p.h.

Total Weight, in Working Order................. 198,500 lbs.

Diesel Engine, one, Normally Aspirated .... 6 cyl.

Supplies:

    Lubricating Oil .... 165 gals.

    Fuel Oil .... 650 gals.

    Cooling Water .... 250 gals.

    Sand .... 30 cu. ft.

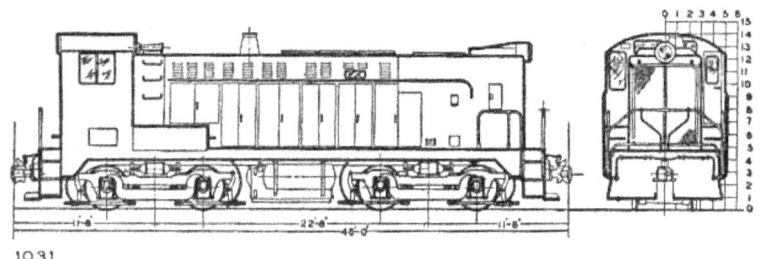

Figure 3

1000 H. P. SWITCHER

GENERAL SPECIFICATIONS

Driving Wheels, 4 pairs ....40 inches

Gear Ratio 14:68

Maximum Speed Restriction ....60 m.p.h.

Total Weight, in Working Order..................235,000 lbs.

Diesel Engine, one, Supercharged......................6 cyl.

Supplies:

    Lubricating Oil ....170 gals.

    Fuel Oil ....650 gals.

    Cooling Water ....250 gals.

    Sand ....30 cu. ft.

GENERAL DESCRIPTION

These locomotives are designed with all the flexibility of operation necessary for switching service. Road switchers, as the name implies, are in all essentials road locomotives. Yard switchers, although not road jobs, have sufficient weight, power and speed to handle moderate train movements where service requirements may extend beyond yard limits.

The engine on a Diesel-Electric locomotive drives a direct connected main generator which delivers electric power to traction motors geared to the truck axle. The electrical transmission, through "Auto-Load" control, protects the Diesel engine from overloads, provides maximum smooth acceleration and compensates for temperature variations, so that full engine horsepower is always available.

Most of the manual controls for the locomotive are located in the cab which is illustrated on the next page. The engine is started by means of the engine start button which connects the main generator to the storage battery. The generator acts as a motor while cranking the engine. After the engines are started, the principal controls for the locomotive are as follows:

1. Throttle—Controlling power and speed.
2. Reverse Lever—Controlling the direction of travel.
3. Automatic Brake Valve.
4. Independent Brake Valve.
   (Standard air braking equipment is used.)

The battery switch and traction motor cutout switches are the only manually controlled switches in the standard equipment cabinet shown on page 7. They are on a 75 volt control circuit. However, high voltage power equipment is also mounted in this cabinet. See Safety Note on page 7.

Crews should be familiar with such automatic protective equipment as Overspeed Stop (page 26), Lube Oil Pressure Switch (page 23) and Fuses or Breakers (page 29).

An auxiliary generator charges the battery, energizes the control circuits and supplies the exciter 4-pole field at a regulated constant voltage. The exciter, in turn, furnishes main generator field excitation.

LOCOMOTIVE — OPERATING CONTROLS

ENGINEER'S POSITION

Figure 4

1. THROTTLE
2. REVERSE LEVER
3. AUTOMATIC BRAKE VALVE
4. INDEPENDENT BRAKE VALVE
5. SANDER VALVE
6. BRAKE PIPE AND CYLINDER PRESSURE GAUGE
7. MAIN AND EQUALIZING RESERVOIR PRESSURE GAUGE
8. LOAD AMMETER
9. BATTERY PARALLEL LIGHT
10. START BUTTON
11. HEATER FAN SWITCH
12. HOOD LIGHT SWITCH
13. AUXILIARY GENERATOR SWITCH
14. BATTERY AMMETER
15. WATER TEMPERATURE GAUGE
16. FUEL OIL PRESSURE GAUGE
17. LUBE OIL PRESSURE GAUGE (at engine)
18. LUBE OIL PRESSURE GAUGE (at turbocharger)
19. CONTROL AND LIGHTING PUSH-BUTTON SWITCHES
20. HEATER RHEOSTAT
21. WHEEL SLIP BUZZER
22. CONTROL AIR PRESSURE GAUGE
23. WHISTLE VALVE
24. FRONT HEADLIGHT SWITCH
25. REAR HEADLIGHT SWITCH
26. WINDSHIELD WIPER VALVE

NOT SHOWN:
    BELL RINGER VALVE (below item 5)
    DOUBLE HEADING COCK (behind item 5)
    EMERGENCY FUEL CUTOFF PULL-RING (behind operator's arm rest)

BALDWIN PAGE 7

ELECTRICAL EQUIPMENT CABINET

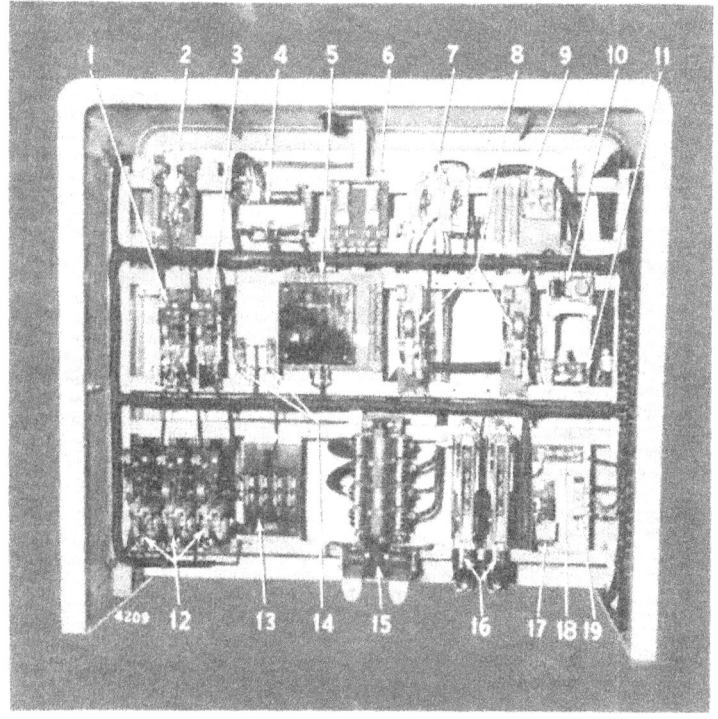

Figure 5

1. BATTERY PARALLEL CONTACTOR
2. TRACTION MOTOR FIELD SHUNT RELAY
3. REVERSE CURRENT CONTACTOR
4. REVERSE CURRENT RELAY
5. VOLTAGE REGULATOR
6. WHEEL SLIP RELAY
7. BATTERY PARALLEL RELAYS
8. FIELD SHUNTING CONTACTORS
9. GROUND RELAY (if installed)
10. PNEUMATIC THROTTLE SWITCH
11. PNEUMATIC FIELD CONTROL SWITCH
12. STARTING CONTACTORS
13. BATTERY SWITCH
14. TRACTION MOTOR CUTOUT SWITCHES
15. REVERSER
16. PNEUMATIC POWER SWITCHES
17. EXCITER FIELD CONTACTOR
18. AUXILIARY GENERATOR FUSE
19. BATTERY AMMETER SHUNT

SAFETY NOTE—The main power circuits operate at 600 volts, or more. Keep cabinet doors closed. Only qualified personnel should open the doors, and adequate precaution should be observed.

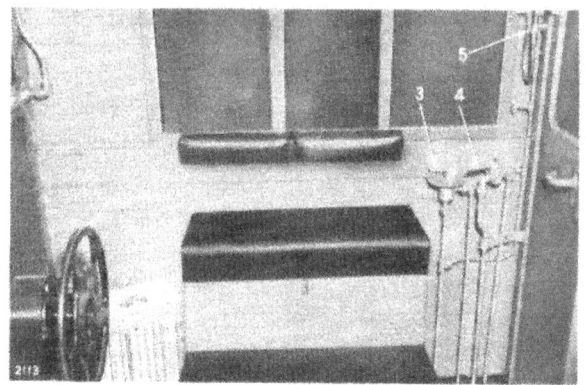

CAB—LEFT SIDE
Figure 6

1. HAND BRAKE
2. HEATER
3. BELL RINGER VALVE
4. WHISTLE VALVE (Installed on left side as optional extra item only.)
5. WINDSHIELD WIPER VALVE

LUBRICATING OIL SYSTEM DETAILS

LUBE OIL PUMP & HEAT EXCHANGER
750 AND 1000 H.P. SWITCHER
Figure 7

1. LUBE OIL FULL FLOW FILTER
2. METAL EDGE TYPE LUBE OIL PRESSURE STRAINER
3. HEAT EXCHANGER
4. LUBE OIL PUMP
5. LUBE OIL SUCTION STRAINER

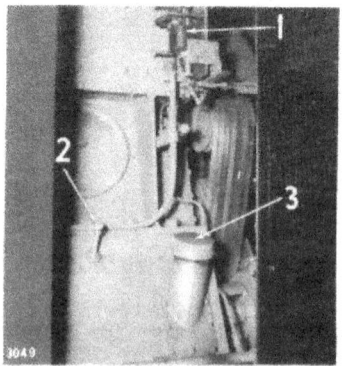

LUBRICATING OIL FILL AND LEVEL GAUGE

Figure 8

1. SHUT-DOWN VALVE
2. OIL LEVEL GAUGE
3. OIL FILL

BALDWIN PAGE 9

FUEL OIL SYSTEM DETAILS

FUEL OIL SUPPLY PUMP

Figure 9

1. FUEL OIL PRESSURE FILTER
2. FUEL OIL SUCTION STRAINER
3. FUEL OIL SUPPLY PUMP
4. RELIEF VALVE

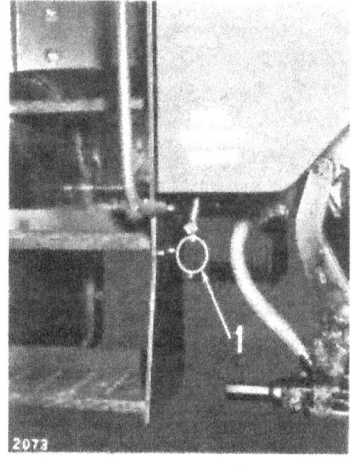

OUTSIDE FUEL CUT-OFF
Figure 10
1. EMERGENCY OUTSIDE FUEL OIL CUT-OFF VALVE PULL RING

FUEL TANK
Figure 11
1. FUEL OIL FILL
2. FUEL GAUGE

LOCOMOTIVE OPERATION

Locomotive Operation is discussed under the following main headings:

		PAGE
I	Preliminary	10
II	Starting Diesel Engine	10
III	Pumping Air	11
IV	Moving Locomotive	12
V	Inspection During Operation	14
VI	Cutting Out Traction Motors	15
VII	Stopping Locomotive	16
VIII	Reversing Locomotive	16
IX	Shutting Down Locomotive	17
X	Shutting Down Engine in Emergency	17
XI	Multiple Unit Operation	17
XII	Procedure for Changing Operating Cab	18
XIII	Pusher or Double Heading Service	19

I. Preliminary:

A. Check the following supplies:
1. Fuel oil.
2. Engine crankcase and governor oil.
3. Air compressor crankcase oil.
4. Engine cooling water.
5. Sand.
6. Heating boiler, (if a boiler is installed).

B. Check for any leaks in fuel, water and lubricating oil piping.

C. Light lamps, if required, by closing the corresponding switches on the control stand. On most locomotives, no lights but the cab lights will burn until the battery switch in the equipment cabinet is closed.

D. Inspect the engine, generator and other machinery for rags, tools, etc., that may have been accidentally left near moving parts.

II. Starting the Diesel Engine:

A. Close battery switch. (Check that M.U. switch, if in-

BALDWIN

installed, is in single unit position "S", if operating alone. See page 17 for multiple unit operation.)
B. Put the throttle in the "idle" position.
C. Insert reverse lever. Put it in the "off" position.
D. Close the control switch. The fuel supply pump should start, and a pressure of 25 lbs. minimum should be indicated on the fuel oil pressure gauges. If pump does not run, check control switch fuse. If pump runs and no pressure is indicated, check fuel supply or emergency fuel cut-off valve at the fuel tank and reset if necessary.
E. Press the engine start button. If the engine does not turn, release the button immediately. See page 32. If the engine turns, hold button in until the engine fires **and** a lubricating oil pressure of 19 lbs. shows on the gauge. Releasing the start button before the required pressure is indicated, permits the engine shut-down device to stop the engine. If engine does not fire, do not hold button in more than 10 seconds because continued cranking will run down the battery.
F. Check the lubricating oil pressure gauge. It should register a pressure between 60 and 70 lbs. when engine is operating at rated speed and normal operating temperatures have been reached.
G. Close the auxiliary generator switch at engineer's position to establish normal field excitation and charge the battery.
H. Let the engine idle until the water temperature reaches 120° F.

III. Pumping Air:
A. As the engine runs, the air compressor will pump air into the main reservoirs. Check the main reservoir air pressure to be sure the compressor stops pumping when the governor cut-out setting of 140 lbs. is reached.
B. Air may be pumped at a higher rate if desired by

bringing the engine speed above idling as follows:
1. Leave the reverse lever in the "off" position.
2. Increase the throttle setting, speeding up the engine and the compressor, until the pumping rate desired is reached. Never move the throttle more than ¾ open for this purpose.
3. Return the throttle to the "idle" position when air pressure gauge registers required pressure.

C. Be sure the air compressor resumes pumping when the main reservoir pressure drops to the lower governor setting of 125 lbs.

D. Check the control air pressure on the gauge in the cab. It should be 70 lbs.

IV. Moving the Locomotive:

A. With the throttle in the "idle" position and the reverser "off", check that:
1. The traction motor cut-out switches in the control cabinet are closed.
2. The traction motor blowers are operating properly.
3. The radiator fan is operating. It is belt driven from the engine. See page 24.
4. The automatic and independent air brakes apply and release properly.
5. On locomotives equipped for multiple operation check the multiple unit switch in the equipment cabinet, making sure it is in the "single unit" position. (See page 17 for multiple operation.)

B. Move the reverse lever to the "forward" or "reverse" position according to the direction the locomotive is to travel.

C. Release brakes and move the throttle slowly from the "idle" position until a current flow shows on the load ammeter. If the train is not too heavy nor the grade severe the locomotive will move. If the locomotive does not move, return the throttle to "idle" immediately. See page 32.

BALDWIN

D. When the meter registers current and the train starts to move, slowly move the throttle to the position required for the train acceleration desired.

E. The throttle should be moved slowly to prevent the wheels from slipping. If the wheels should slip, the wheel slip buzzer will sound and the Diesel engine speed will automatically decrease until the slipping stops. If wheels slip again, retard the throttle until wheel slip stops.

F. The high starting tractive effort of the Diesel-Electric locomotive makes use of sand seldom necessary.
CAUTION: Do not apply sand while the wheels are slipping. Always use sand sparingly.
If sand is necessary, it may be applied as follows:
1. On locomotives equipped with hand sanding, moving the sanding lever to the "forward" position will apply sand in front of both trucks; and moving the lever to the "reverse" position will apply sand to the rear of both trucks.
2. On locomotives equipped with electric sanding, depressing the sander foot switch will sand either the front or the rear of both trucks, depending on the position of the reverse lever.

G. As train speed increases the traction motor fields are automatically weakened by shunting the field windings with resistance, rendering it possible to run at higher speeds. Amperage increases at time of shunting.

H. LOAD LIMIT. Excessive loads will heat electrical equipment enough to result in serious damage and failure. The damage may not be apparent immediately but can cause failure later. Electrical apparatus will safely carry an overload for a limited time if maximum allowable temperature has not been reached. The following table gives typical time-load limitations if the equipment has not recently been subject to heavy loads and heating. Typical examples of operating requirements in this respect are:

Overload is Permitted

1. If the engine has idled for 15 minutes or more just previous to the overload.
2. If, during the preceding hour, the locomotive has averaged about half of continuous rating.

No Overload is Permitted

1. If the locomotive has been operating at or near continuous rating for one hour or more.
2. If an overload has existed for the period of time specified in the accompanying table.

When the time limit is reached for any overload, the engine must be idled for 15 minutes to cool the equipment unless the train can continue at full engine speed at or below the continuous rating. No overload capacity exists at any other amperage above continuous rating. The generator may operate continuously at full engine speed at, or below, the continuous rating. The crew should pay careful attention to load limits in any abnormal operation for which the railroad has no established tonnage ratings, as when a traction motor is cut-out (See VI following).

TIME-LOAD LIMITS

Time Limit	Amperes
Continuous Rating	1050
Overloads	
30 Minutes	1100
20 Minutes	1150
10 Minutes	1300
5 Minutes	1450

V. Inspections During Operation:

A. Check gauges frequently. Investigate any great deviation from normal.

>Lube oil pressure, engine—Normal 65 lbs. (at rated speed).

BALDWIN PAGE 15

>   Lube oil pressure, turbocharger—Normal 20 lbs. to 30 lbs.
>   Water temperature—about 150° to 190° F.

- B. Rotate the handles on the metal edge lubricating oil strainer two full turns every 4 hours. This strainer is located in the radiator compartment and is accessible through a door provided in this compartment. (Figure 7.)

- C. Check the cooling water level on the gauge at expansion tank every 8 hours. Level must be maintained so that water is visible at all times in the gauge glass.

- D. Check the lubricating oil level once every 8 hours, with the engine stopped. It must be maintained above the "low" mark on the bayonet gauge.

- E. Drain the main air reservoirs once every 8 hours.

- F. Check battery ammeter. It should never show a discharge when engine is running. Report such condition to Maintenance. The high charging rate after starting the engine will decrease and approach zero as the battery becomes fully charged.

- G. Make periodic visual inspection of equipment under the locomotive for loose or dragging parts.

- H. Investigate any unusual noises or odors and report to maintainer.

VI. Cutting Out a Traction Motor:

- A. Should a failure occur in a traction motor it may be taken out of service by opening the traction motor cut-out switch in the equipment cabinet. Do not open this switch while power is on.
    1. Return the throttle to "idle" position and put the reverse lever in "off" position.
    2. Open the proper traction motor cutout switch. No. 1 switch cuts out No. 1 and No. 3 motors.

No. 2 switch cuts out No. 2 and No. 4 motors. Motors are numbered in sequence from front to rear.

B. When operating with a set of traction motors cut-out, do not exceed ½ of the normal current rating on the load ammeter. Current is automatically reduced without corresponding reduction in throttle setting.

NOTE: Do not try to rerail a locomotive under its own power, as serious damage may result to the traction motor from spinning the wheels. However, if only one pair of wheels is derailed it is possible to rerail the locomotive under its own power by cutting out the motor driving the derailed wheels.

VII. Stopping the Locomotive:

A. Move the throttle to the "idle" position.

B. Apply the brakes.
   1. Do not use the independent air brake to stop a heavy train; use the automatic brake.
   2. Never apply brakes unless throttle is in "idle" position, as this may result in an overload.

C. If the locomotive is to be left standing temporarily,
   1. Put the reverse lever in the "off" position.
   2. Apply the hand brake.

VIII. Reversing the Locomotive:

A. Bring the locomotive to a full stop as just outlined in section VII.

B. Move the reverse lever for operation in the **opposite direction.**

C. Release the brakes.

D. **Move the throttle slowly toward the full speed position.**

CAUTION: Never move the reverse lever while the locomotive is in motion as this may result in serious damage to the electrical equipment.

IX. Shutting Down the Locomotive:
   A. Let the engine idle for at least ten minutes.
   B. Open the control switch.
   C. Open the auxiliary generator switch.
   D. Open the main battery switch.
   E. Set the hand brake and release the air brakes.
   F. Turn off all lights.
   G. Remove reverse lever.
   H. If the locomotive will be exposed to freezing temperatures take the necessary precautions (page 24).

X. Shutting Down Engine in an Emergency:
   A. Open control switch.
   B. Pull the red emergency fuel cut-off valve handle in the right rear corner of the cab, or on the outside of the locomotive at the right rear corner (Fig. 10).

It will be necessary to reset the fuel cut-off valve before starting the engine. Put the throttle in the "idle" position, and put the reverse lever in the "off" position before restarting.

XI. Multiple Unit Operation:
   A. Couple the units together and connect the air lines and jumpers, making sure that each plug is pushed all the way into the receptacle and locked in place.
   B. Open the cocks at the end of the air lines on both locomotives in the following sequence: throttle line, main reservoir line, equalizing pipe and train line.
   C. On trailing or non-controlling unit.
      1. Close the double heading cock on the brake pedestal.
      2. Put the automatic brake in "holding" position.
      3. Put independent brake in the "release" position.
      4. Put the "Transfer Valve Operating Cock" (located on the Control Stand) in the "trailing" position.
      5. Put the throttle in the "idle" position.

6. Put the reverse lever in the "off" position and remove the handle.
7. Close the multiple unit switch in the equipment cabinet to the "M. U." (Multiple Unit) position.
8. Close the main battery switch in the equipment cabinet.
9. Open "control switch" and lock in place.
10. Release the hand brake.

D. On the leading or controlling unit.
   1. Make sure the multiple unit switch is closed in the "S" (Single Unit) position.
   2. Close main battery switch.
   3. Put the "Transfer Valve Operating Cock" (located on the control stand) in the "lead or dead" position on the controlling unit.
   4. Open double heading cock on brake pedestal.
   5. Close "control switch".

E. Start the engines as previously outlined on page 10. It will be necessary to start the engine in the trailing unit from its cab after starting the engine in the leading unit. However, in the trailing unit, leave the control switch open.

F. Close the auxiliary generator switches.

G. The locomotives may now be operated in the same manner as a single unit. The sander foot switch will apply sand to the front or rear of both trucks on both units as determined by the position of the reverser.

H. The cock located above the DKR Distributing valve under the skirt of the cab is to remain open at all times except when the locomotive is to be towed dead in a train at which time it is to be closed.

XII. Procedure for **Changing Operating Cab:**
   A. In the cab which has been controlling.
      1. Make at least a 20 pound reduction with automatic brake valve.

BALDWIN

   2. Place double heading cock in cutout position.
   3. Move automatic brake valve handle to "holding" position and independent brake to "release" position.
   4. Move "Transfer Valve Operating Cock" to the "trailing" position

B. In the cab which will be controlling.
   1. Move independent brake valve handle to full "application" position, move automatic brake valve handle to "running" position.
   2. Cut in double heading cock, horizontal position.
   3. Move "Transfer Valve Operating Cock" to "lead" position.
   4. Push in control button on throttle stand.
   5. Change multiple unit switch from "M.U." to "S" position.

C. Return to the former controlling cab.
   1. Change multiple unit switch from "S" to "M.U." position.
   2. Pull out control button and lock in position.
      The units are now ready for multiple operation. If not, check control fuse.

XIII. Pusher or Double Heading Service:

A. Close the double heading cock and place handles of both brake valves in the running position.

B. On locomotives equipped for multiple unit operation, put the "Transfer Valve Operating Cock" (located on the control stand) in the "lead or dead" position.

The power controls may then be used in the normal fashion and the brakes will be controlled on both units by the leading locomotive.

FUEL OIL SYSTEM

Fuel is drawn from the tank under the center of the locomotive through the emergency fuel cut-off valve and the suction strainer by the motor driven fuel oil supply pump. The fuel tank may be filled on either side of the locomotive. Fill the tank slowly and watch the level gauge at top of tank to avoid overflowing. The pump then forces the fuel through the pressure filter to the fuel header supplying the injection pumps. A pressure relief valve holds the fuel pressure in the header to 25 lbs., bypassing the excess fuel back to the tank. The supply pump is protected against pressure by a relief valve connected to its discharge.

The pressure filter cartridges should be renewed every fifteen days. The suction strainer should be cleaned weekly.

ENGINE SHUT-DOWN DEVICE

An electrically controlled engine shut-down device protects the Diesel engine against low lubricating oil pressure. The purchaser may also specify protection against hot cooling system, as an optional extra item. The device is operated by fuel oil pressure and automatically moves the fuel control shaft to the stop position when the protective devices function.

A three-way magnetic valve is supplied with fuel oil from the fuel supply pump. This valve is energized when the lubricating oil pressure is over 15 lbs. and the cooling water temperature is less than 190° F. The switches in the control circuit, Fig. 12, are closed at such times. (When starting the Diesel engine, the lube oil pressure switch closes initially at 19 lbs.) When energized, oil flows through the valve to the shut-down cylinder, releasing the fuel control shaft and allowing it to act according to the demands of the governor. When the lubricating oil pressure falls below 15 lbs. or the engine overheats, the valve is de-energized and oil is released from the shut-down cylinder. A spring in the cylinder then forces the piston and fuel control shaft to the stop position, which shuts down the engine.

When the engine start button is held in, these protective switches are by-passed so that the engine may be started.

BALDWIN

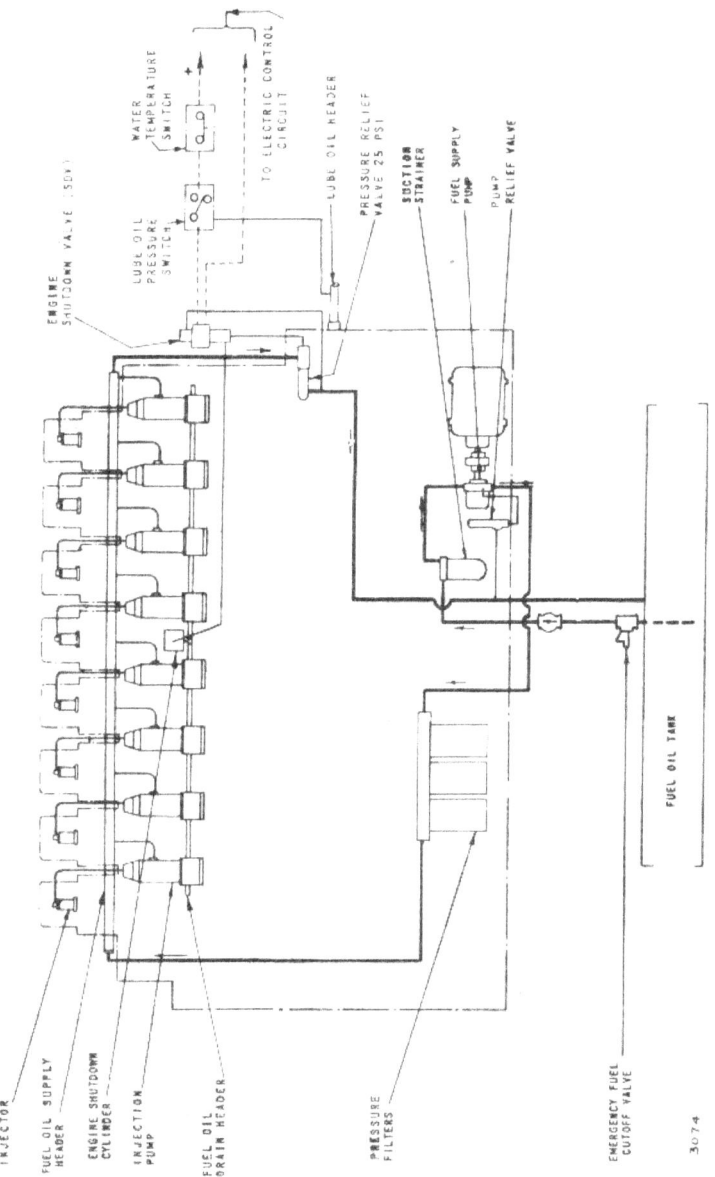

Diagram of Fuel Oil System

Figure 12

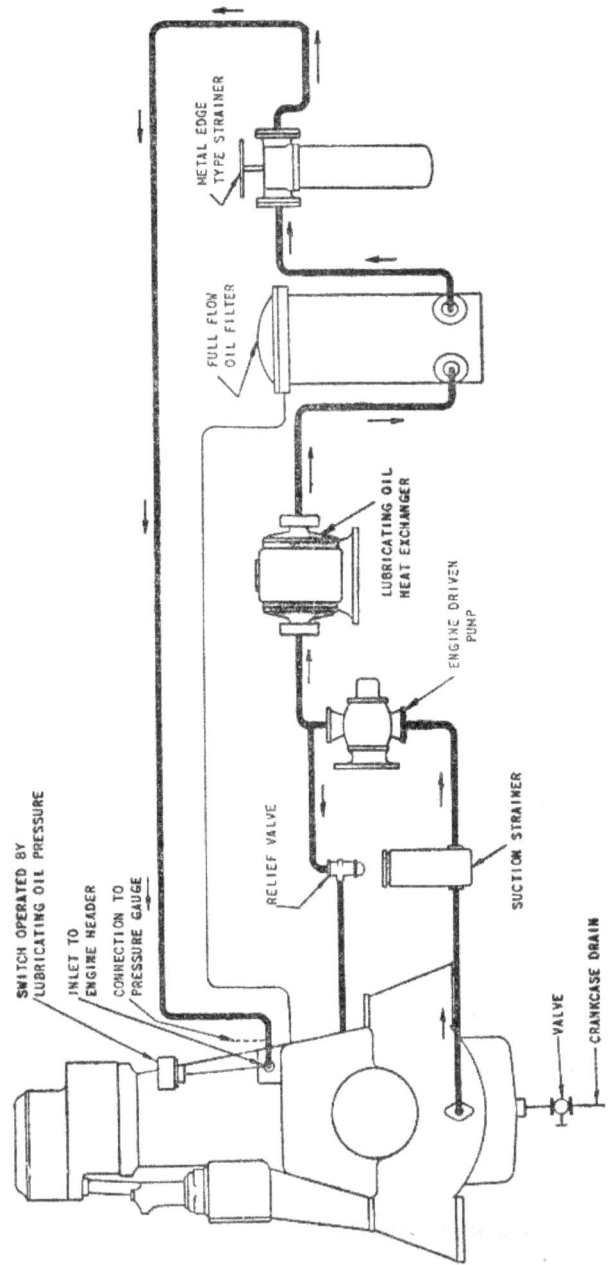

LUBRICATING OIL SYSTEM
750 AND 1000 H.P. SWITCHERS
FIGURE 13

BALDWIN

LUBRICATING OIL SYSTEM

The lubricating oil is drawn from the sump, formed by the bedplate of the engine, through a suction strainer by the engine driven pump. The pump forces the oil through an oil filter, a metal edge oil strainer, and a heat exchanger. (See Figure 7.) The oil is then delivered to the engine header, which distributes the oil to all parts of engine requiring lubrication.

MAINTENANCE

The oil level in the sump should be checked daily and must be maintained above the "Low" mark. The handle on the metal edge type strainer must be rotated every four hours.

To fill the crankcase, pour the proper type of oil through the filler pipe. Fill to the "Full" mark on the bayonet gauge. To drain oil from the engine, open the drain valve and remove the plugs from the bottom of the camshaft trough. Drain the oil into a suitable container. Also, be sure to drain the strainers, the filter and the heat exchanger, when changing crankcase oil.

Refer to Maintenance Bulletin No. MBD-131 for lube oil filter maintenance instructions.

LUBE OIL PRESSURE SWITCH

The lube oil pressure switch is a protective device which is kept closed by oil pressure (See Figure 13), but opens when the lubricating system fails from loss of pressure. When this switch is closed, shutdown valve SDV is energized which is necessary to maintain the fuel supply to the engine (See Figure 12). When the switch opens, SDV is de-energized and the engine stops, as just described under engine shutdown device in the text on the Fuel Oil System.

ENGINE COOLING WATER SYSTEM

Water is circulated through the engine, heat exchanger and cooling radiator by an engine driven pump, see Figure 14. An expansion tank vented to the atmosphere through an overflow pipe acts as a reservoir for maintaining the system full. The water level in the expansion tank must be maintained above the "low" mark on the gauge. Check every 8 hours.

To fill the system, add water through the connection located over No. 1 truck on right side of the locomotive. Run water until water spills through the overflow pipe. The system can be filled through the filler on the roof near the front, but it is not recommended because of the danger of trapping air in the system. If the engine overheats because of low water level, idle the engine and add hot water if possible. If it is necessary to use cold water, it should be added very slowly.

If the locomotive is to be left standing exposed to freezing temperature, it will be necessary to drain the cooling system or use an outside source of steam to prevent freezing. If a steam source is available, connect it to the drain pipe through a check valve so that the water can not back up into the steam line. Open the drain valve enough to allow steam to enter the system. To drain the system, open the drain valve (Figure 14), and also the drain cock on the underside of the heat exchanger. The heat exchanger will not drain properly unless its drain cock is opened.

AUTOMATIC TEMPERATURE CONTROL
WITH AN ENGINE DRIVEN RADIATOR FAN

The cooling water system incorporates a fan, V-belt driven from the engine, and continuously engaged. Automatically controlled shutters remain closed until water temperature reaches 160 degrees, at which time the shutters open. The shutters close when water temperature drops to 153 degrees. Temperature may rise to 190° or 200° F. with safety, at which point a water temperature switch (Figure 12, if applied) opens automatically to shut down the engine (See page 20).

If the shutters fail to open, the manual control valve should be opened. It is located on a stiffening member just inside the left front hood door.

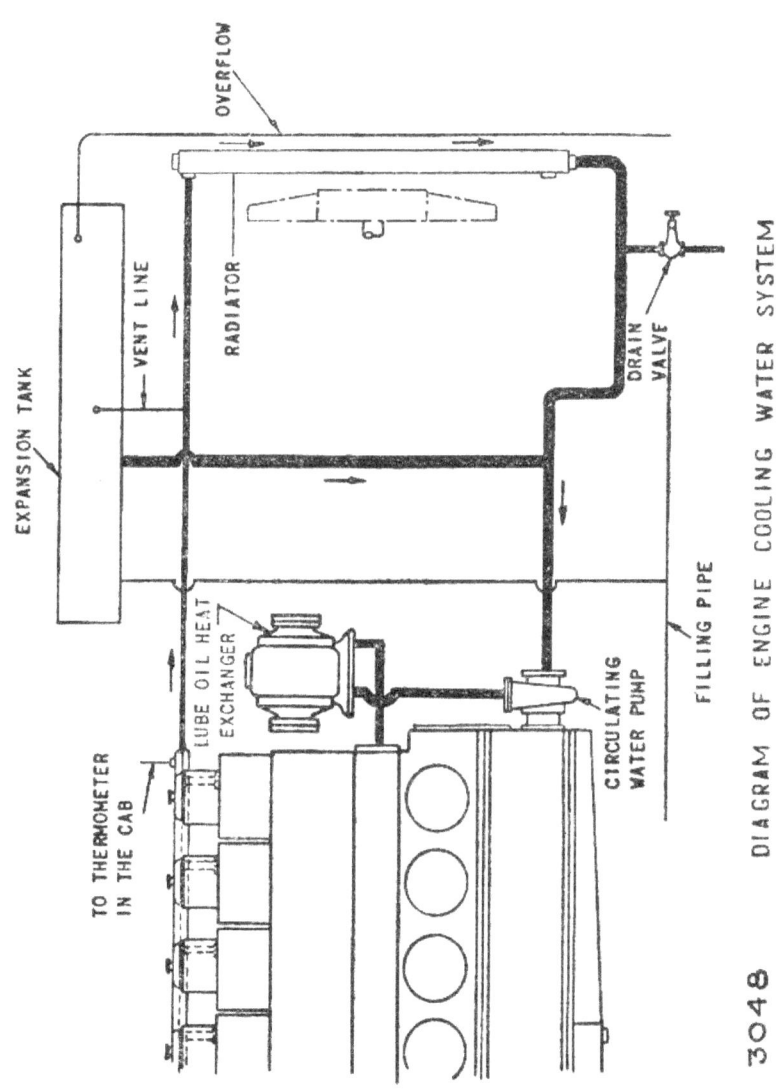

Cooling Water System

750 AND 1000 H.P. Switcher

Figure 14

ENGINE OVERSPEED CONTROL

The engine is prevented from exceeding a specific safe RPM through action of an overspeed stop. This appliance, situated on the front of the camshaft casing at the generator end of the engine, is a spring loaded tripping device, set to trip at a predetermined camshaft speed. The tripping operation actuates a plunger which moves the fuel control shaft to the "No Fuel" position and stops the engine. Before starting engine again, the overspeed stop must be reset.

CONTROL AIR SYSTEM

The air compressor operates whenever the engine runs. The governor cutout is set so that pressure is not built up beyond 140 pounds in the main reservoir. Pumping is resumed when pressure drops to 125 pounds. The standard braking system is supplied from this reservoir.

RESETTING OVERSPEED STOP

FIGURE 15

1. RESET BAR. PULL DOWN TO RESET OVERSPEED STOP

Pneumatic controls are supplied from an auxiliary reservoir at 70 pounds pressure. This reservoir is fed from the main reservoir through a reducing valve.

The following equipment is operated by the 70 pound control air pressure:

>Reverser
>Power Switches
>Pneumatic Throttle Control System
>>Throttle Switch
>>Field Control Switch
>>Governor Actuator
>
>Shutter Control System

ELECTRICAL SYSTEM

An electrical drive is the most practical means of transmitting Diesel engine power to the driving wheels, and electro-pneumatic controls provide the simplest means of handling both the propulsion motors and the auxiliary equipment. Normal operations are controlled by a throttle, a reverser lever, and a braking system which is handled in about the same manner as on other prevalent types of railroad motive power. After the manually operated switches are set for normal operation, and the engine started as previously described herein, the various operations controlling power, speed, field shunting, engine cooling, etc., occur automatically.

Operating men should have some fundamental knowledge of the electrical system. They are then more competent to handle the controls, watch indicating instruments for prevention of trouble, and meet non-routine operating conditions when they arise.

Most of the instruments and routine controls are mounted on panels in front of the engineer. An illustration of the inside of the equipment cabinet near the front of this book shows most of the other electrical control equipment on the locomotive. These controls should be thoroughly understood before investigating or repairing any trouble. There is high voltage on much of this equipment and no attempt should be made to enter the cabinet without taking proper safety precautions.

The main generator supplies high voltage power to the traction motors. See Control System Diagram Fig. 16. The auxiliary generator charges the battery and supplies low voltage power (about 75 volts) to the lighting and control circuits and the 4-pole exciter field circuit. When more than one Diesel engine is controlled from one controller, the only electrical connections between units are low voltage control circuits.

The principal types of control equipment function as follows.

Relays—A relay is a coil which opens or closes a set of comparatively light-duty contacts (generally in a controlling circuit). The coil may be in either the high or low voltage circuit and may be adjusted to pick-up or drop-out at various voltages, and calibrated to respond to varying operating conditions. As the name implies, it relays an impulse to other equipment (mostly contactors), and more than one contactor may be controlled by a single relay.

Contactors—A contactor is a coil-operated set of contacts (generally heavy-duty, and in the circuit being controlled). Its closed or open positions generally depend on whether it is energized or de-energized. There is usually no adjustment for intermediate voltages or currents, because the more sensitive relays are used for such purposes. Light-duty contacts on a contactor are called interlocks which are described in the next paragraph.

Interlocks—An interlock is an auxiliary contact operated by a cam or by a mechanical linkage. Its open or closed position depends on the position of the main contacts. It is frequently necessary to prevent the closing of a certain circuit (call it "a") unless a certain other circuit (call it "b") is open (or closed, depending on design or sequence). An interlock on a contactor in "b" can be wired to control the circuit leading to "a" to achieve the desired results. They generally follow the cam by spring action. The chief concern to the operator is that sluggish or faulty action can cause faulty locomotive operation.

Electro-pneumatic Valve—An electro-pneumatic valve (or

magnet valve) consists of an electrical coil in a controlling circuit which controls valves for the pneumatic operation of certain equipment. For example the reverser and the power switches are pneumatically operated by a valve which is built into the equipment. Control air pressure is maintained from the main air reservoir, but at a lower pressure.

Breaker-type Switch—Some manually operated switches open automatically when overloaded, and should be checked if the circuits involved are not functioning. They must be moved to full "off" position before being reclosed.

Fuses—A burned-out fuse in the auxiliary generator circuit, or behind the control pushbutton will interfere with the operation of the locomotive. Various lighting circuits are fused independently in order to localize trouble as much as possible.

Voltage Regulator and Battery Protection—A voltage regulator holds the auxiliary generator voltage constant over the normal speed range of the Diesel engine. It is set slightly above battery voltage so the battery will receive a charge if necessary. The battery is protected against discharge through an idle or defective auxiliary generator by a reverse current relay which opens a contactor in the circuit if a reverse current flows. This contactor closes automatically any time auxiliary generator voltage exceeds battery voltage. Operators should not change the adjustment or setting of this equipment.

CONTROL SYSTEM

A diagram of the principal equipment in the control system is shown in Fig. 16. Many details are purposely omitted so that the essential relationships are more easily understood. The master controller consists principally of a throttle and a reverse lever. A condensed sequence of operations follows:

Stage of Operation	Electrical Action	Pneumatic Action
Starting	Main generator is connected to battery (wires not shown in diagram). It acts as motor to turn or crank the engine. Other generator connections are open.	None.
Engine Idling	After starting and closing auxiliary generator switch, auxiliary generator is connected to battery. Main generator field and exciter field energized by automatic closing of field contactors, if fans are electrically driven.	None.
Reverse Lever set to change direction.	Reverser magnet valve connections established but not energized until throttle is advanced in next step.	Operating cylinder moves reverser when reverser valves are energized (after the throttle is advanced).
Throttle Advance	Magnet valves in reverser and traction motor contactors (P switches) are energized.	Fuel supply increased and engine speeds up. See pneumatic lines on diagram. P switches close as soon as their magnet valves are energized.
Running at high speed.	Traction motor fields are shunted by: (a) Field shunt relays (FS) close at a set generator voltage, which energizes the field shunting contactors (M). (b) M contactors close to connect the field shunts.	Same as above, but no additional action.
Throttle retard.	Reverse of above.	Reverse of above.
Wheels slip.	Wheel slip relays pickup. They are sensitive to unbalanced voltage conditions at the traction motors. They close a circuit which energizes a valve in throttle line.	Throttle line air pressure is reduced. Fuel supply reduced. Pressure automatically restored when slip stops.

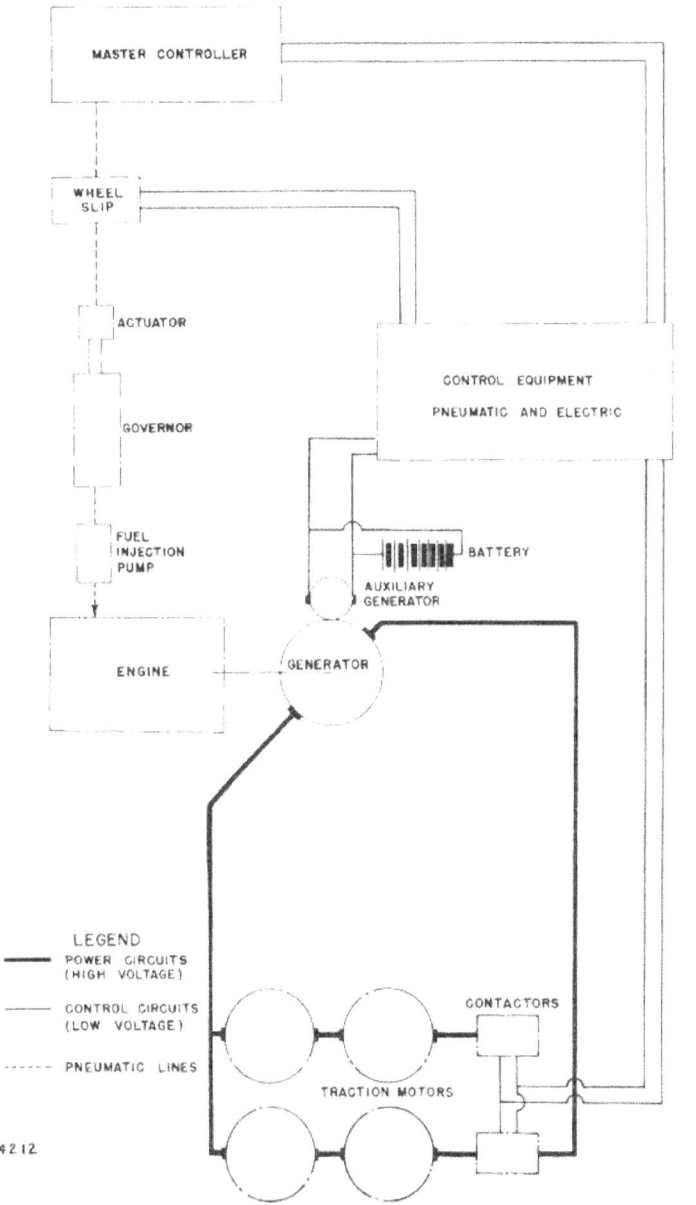

Control System Diagram
Figure 16

OPERATING DIFFICULTIES AND CAUSES

I. **Engine Does Not Turn When Starting Button Is Pressed:**
   A. Control switch open,—or fuse burned out.
   B. Battery switch open
   C. Multiple unit switch not in the correct position, if locomotive is equipped for multiple operation.

II. **Engine Turns But Does Not Fire, or Continue Running After Releasing the Starting Button:**
   A. Fuel tank empty.
   B. Emergency fuel cut-out valve is tripped. Reset.
   C. Overspeed stop has been tripped. Reset.
   D. Releasing start button before lubricating oil pressure has built up to 19 lbs.
   E. Low fuel oil pressure.
   F. Insufficient oil supply in the governor.

III. **Engine Does Not Respond to Throttle Setting:**
   A. Low control air pressure
      1. Low main reservoir air pressure
      2. Control air cut-out cock closed.
      3. Control air pressure reducing valve sticking. Try tapping it.
   B. Governor linkage disconnected

IV. **Locomotive Does Not Move:**
   A. Reverser not in the "forward" or "reverse" position
   B. Auxiliary generator switch open
   C. Traction motor cut-out switches open
   D. Hand brake still set
   E. Pneumatic throttle switch open

V. **Engine Stops:**
   A. Overspeed stop has tripped. Reset (Fig. 15). Notify maintainer if it continues to trip.
   B. Low lubricating oil pressure, causing the engine shutdown device to operate

C. High water temperature, causing the engine shut-down device to operate (when provided on the locomotive)
D. Emergency fuel cut-out valve has been tripped. Reset
E. Fuel tank empty

VI. Low Fuel Oil Pressure:
A. Fuel tank empty
B. Emergency fuel cut-out valve tripped. Reset
C. Sticking relief valves. Try tapping them
D. Faulty pump

VII. Low Lubricating Oil Pressure:
A. Low oil level
B. Clogged pressure strainer. Turn the handle on top of the strainer two revolutions in the clockwise direction
C. Sticking relief valves. Try tapping them
D. Hot or diluted oil.

VIII. Engine Overheats:
A. Low water level.
B. Faulty radiator shutter control. See page 24.
C. Radiator fans not functioning properly. Check belt drive.

IX. Air Pressure Too High or Too Low:
A. Compressor governor cut-out cock closed
B. Compressor governor sticking. Try tapping it

X. Battery Ammeter Shows Discharge (Engine Running):
A. Auxiliary Generator Switch open
B. Auxiliary Generator Fuse burned out
C. Poor contacts on battery contactor or reverse current relay.

NOTE: Always notify maintainer as soon as possible when any operating difficulty is experienced.

Notify maintainer *immediately* if the trouble can not be corrected by the above suggestions.

©2011 Periscope Film LLC
All Rights Reserved
ISBN #978-1-935700-62-3
www.PeriscopeFilm.com

www.ingramcontent.com/pod-product-compliance
Lightning Source LLC
Chambersburg PA
CBHW060646050426
42451CB00010B/1219